D1174792

An Introduction to

# Wallpaper

The Original Manufacture Warehouse:

ABRAHAM PRICE, makes and sells the true sorts of FIGUR'D *Paper Hangings Wholesale and Retale*, IN PIECES OF TWELVE YARDS LONG; IN IMITATION OF Irish Stitch, Flower'd Sprigs and Branches: Others Yard-wide in Imitation of Marble, and other colour'd Wainscots, fit for the *Hangings of Parlours, Dining-Rooms, and Staircases*: *And a Curious Sort of Imboss'd Work Resembling Caffaws, and Bed Damasks; with other Things of Curious* FIGURES AND COLOURS; CLOTH TAPESTRY HANGINGS ETC). All *which* are distinguish'd *from any* Pretenders *by these* Words. *at* ý *end of each Piece* The Blue Paper Manufacture.

1
A trade-label engraved by John Sturt (1658–1730).
Early 18th century, English.
The label shows the flock wallpaper with the same pattern as the one from
Ivy House (plate 12).
The label is in the Ambrose Heal collection at the British Museum.

*Reproduced by courtesy of the British Museum*

An Introduction to

# Wallpaper

Jean Hamilton

*Department of Prints and Drawings*
*Victoria and Albert Museum*

LONDON: HER MAJESTY'S STATIONERY OFFICE

Series editor Julian Berry
Designed by HMSO Graphic Design
Printed in England for Her Majesty's Stationery Office

ISBN 0 11 290386 X
Dd 696418 C65

*Acknowledgements*
My thanks are due to Anne Buddle for arranging the photography, and
especially to Sally Chappell for some excellent photographs of some
difficult subjects.
*Jean Hamilton* 16 November 1981

*Glossary of Printing Terms*

| | |
|---|---|
| Etching | An intaglio method in which the lines are bitten by acid on a metal plate |
| Flexography | Specialised form of relief printing in which aniline inks are used on non-absorbent surfaces i.e. flexible rubber plates mounted on cylinders |
| Ink-embossing | Combined method of shallow embossing and inking |
| Rotagravure | Machine photogravure cylinder printing |
| Screenprinting | A method of stencil printing through a silk mesh |
| Wood-engraving | Cutting a design on a wood block, which prints in relief |

HER MAJESTY'S STATIONERY OFFICE

*Government Bookshops*

49 High Holborn, London WC1V 6HB
13a Castle Street, Edinburgh EH2 3AR
Brazennose Street, Manchester M60 8AS
Southey House, Wine Street, Bristol BS1 2BQ
258 Broad Street, Birmingham B1 2HE
80 Chichester Street, Belfast BT1 4JY

*Government Publications are also available through booksellers*

The full range of Museum publications is displayed and sold at
The Victoria & Albert Museum, South Kensington, London SW7 2RL

There is evidence that paper with drawn or printed designs connected with funeral rites was applied to the walls of houses and temples in China AD 206,* but the oldest example of a European wallpaper, made in four 'handed' sections, dates from the first half of the fifteenth century. The pattern, printed from a wood block, was reconstructed from fragments of one of the

*From the accounts of John Hilditch, F.R.G.S.

quarter sections and depicts the sudarium or Holy Cloth of St. Veronica. A German wallpaper [plate 3] with a design also constructed in the same way in quarter sections shows a satyr, a nymph and a boy among grape vines, and is based on a design by Dürer. It is dated c. 1530.

The remains of the earliest English wallpaper [plate 2] were discovered in 1911 decorating the beams of the Hall and Dining Room in the Master's Lodge at Christ's College, Cambridge. The paper had been printed on the backs of several documents of about the year 1509, and was almost certainly the work of Hugo Goes a block cutter of Beverley, for the pomegranate pattern incorporated the Lombardic letter 'H' and a rebus of his name, a goose.

Decorated or pattern papers were produced for several uses, which included linings for chests and coffers, drawers, cupboards and deed boxes, as well as for endpapers of books. But from their size and the nature of their design, some patterns must also have been intended specifically to cover walls. Certain pattern

2

2
Reconstruction of a wallpaper printed from a wood-block.
Original c.1509, English.
Attributed to Hugo Goes.
From the Master's Lodge, Christ's College, Cambridge.
The pattern relates to those of Italian textiles imported into this country in the 15th century. Hugo Goes was a maker of woodcuts and a printer, who had settled in York by 1509. This was the year in which the Master's Lodge was known to have been built. The reconstruction was machine-printed.
E.1783-1914

3
Woodcuts intended as wallpaper designs forming a
repeat.
Original *c.*1530, German.
Attributed to the 'Celtis-Meister' (School of Dürer).
Although the design was previously thought to have
been intended for a textile, recent research has
established its use as a wallpaper (see H. Appuhn and C.
von Reusinger, *Riesenholzschnitte und Papiertapeten der
Renaissance*, Germany, 1976). It was reproduced in the
*Portfolio* of the Dürer Society, 1903.
E.5591,5592-1903

papers exist which have been found both as box or
chest liners and as wallpaper, such as an early seventeenth century paper which lines a charter box belonging
to Abbot's Hospital at Guildford, Surrey, and is of the
same design as a wallpaper recently uncovered in a
closet at the Dower House, Dinton, near Aylesbury.

The majority of 'black and white' woodcut printed
papers of the sixteenth century and early seventeenth
century appear to fall into four main categories. The
first consists of patterns in which coats of arms are
displayed, like the wallpaper from Besford Court,
Worcestershire [plate 4] (a variant of which was used in
a room in the Gate Tower of the Base Court at Hampton

3

6

Court Palace) or the design [plate 5] with the Prince of Wales feathers and initials of Prince Henry, eldest son of James I. The second group consist of patterns based upon the so called 'black stitch'† embroidery [plate 6], and the third group shows scenes of outdoor life [plate 7] related to those depicted in tapestries and cushion covers. The fourth with floral designs, or simple repeats of spots or trellis, were printed over sheets already printed by letterpress [plate 8], which were either proof sheets or leaves from condemned literature such as Hobbes *Leviathan*, ordered by the Bishop of London in 1673 to be 'damasked' or obliterated. These 'black and white' papers survived into the early

eighteenth century as popular decorations, some with sophisticated patterns derived from velvets and brocades [plate 9]. A few have additional hand-painted or stencilled colouring, usually not more than two colours, red and green [plate 10].

The earliest forms of wall decoration were hand-painted or stencilled onto the plaster, and these murals were not superseded by decorated paper, but continued to be used, mainly in country areas, as late as the nineteenth century. Even the simplest woodcut printed on paper was a relatively expensive novelty in the sixteenth and seventeenth centuries, and used only in the larger, wealthier houses.

†Black silk embroidery on a white textile ground.

4

4
A wallpaper printed from wood-blocks.
*c.*1550-75, English.
From Besford Court, Worcestershire. The same pattern was used as a lining-paper in an oak chest of the latter half of the 16th century, and a variation of the pattern has been found in a room in the Gate Tower of the Base Court at Hampton Court Palace, where the mask motifs are replaced by George and the Dragon and figures supporting a crowned rose.
E.3593-1913

5
A lining-paper printed from wood-blocks.
The original is early 17th century, English.
The paper was found in a box dated 1635. H.P. are the initials of
Henry Frederick, Prince of Wales who died in 1612. The design was
reconstructed in a linocut by Wyndham Payne.
E.456,A-C-1951

6
A wallpaper printed from a wood-block.
Early 17th century, English.
The design of a Tudor rose and other flowers is based on the so-called
'black stitch' embroidery.
E.1974-1927

7
A lining-paper or a wallpaper printed from a wood-block.
Late 17th, or early 18th century, English.
The paper was found in an early 17th-century box in the Museum's
collection. It appears to be a contemporary reworking of a lining-
paper from a drawer of a chest belonging to Lord Leverhulme. The
palings and trees in the background are practically identical to those
shown in another decorative paper from Colonial Williamsburg,
U.S.A., which was a companion piece to a wallpaper with a hunting
scene from The Shrubbery, a house at Epsom, Surrey. The American
paper shows a chinoiserie figure walking over a hill. There would
seem to have been a common source, perhaps a painted cloth
hanging, for the three scenes which may have been intended to be
shown in conjunction with one another.
E.405-1968

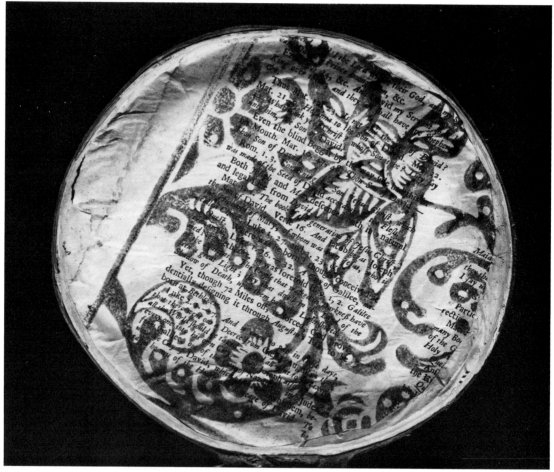

8
A lining-paper printed from a wood-block.
Late 17th, or early 18th century, English.
The paper lines the lid of a 17th-century lace, or kerchief, box. The design is printed on a letterpress sheet with commentaries on the scriptures, probably from a banned publication.
T.447-1976

9
A wallpaper printed from a wood-block.
Early 18th century, English.
From 5 The Grove, Highgate, London. Another slightly cruder version of this pattern of flowers and acanthus leaves was found at Whitmore's, a house in the Dorking Road, Epsom, Surrey.
E.554-1935

10
A wallpaper printed from a wood-block, with stencilled colour.
*c.*1730-40, English.
From Wichenford Court, Worcestershire. The design imitates a damask or a brocade.
E.1082-1978

Borders may have been among the earliest form in which paper was applied on walls which were panelled to within inches of the ceiling. A mid-sixteenth-century lining paper with the Tudor rose pattern repeated could also have been intended as a small frieze [plate 11].

In the late seventeenth century another kind of wallpaper appeared, printed with flock [plate 12]. Throughout the first four centuries of its history wallpaper was primarily an imitative craft, simulating tapestries, silks and brocades for which it offered a cheaper alternative, and for which flock papers were the most effective substitutes. The process of flocking had

been applied to cloth at least since the end of the fifteenth century. An Act of Richard III, in 1483, implied that 'flokkys' were used on poor-quality cloth to cheat the buyer, an early but nefarious use of waste material. François of Rouen is said to have been the first to manufacture flock paper, *c.*1620-30, but the earliest written notice concerning flocking in this country is contained in a patent granted to Jerome Lanyer in 1634 allowing him to affix wool, silk and 'other Materials of divers Cullours uppon Lynnen, Cloath, Silke, Cotten, Leather and other substances'. Though the 'other substances' are unnamed, it is possible that they included paper. The oldest flock in this country with a definite dating, *c.*1680 [plate 13], is from Ivy House, Worcester Cathedral precincts; it was hung in alternating lengths with embossed leather, the latter probably of Netherlandish origin. But whether of Continental origin or not, flocking was developed in England and widely used there during the eighteenth century.

11
A lining-paper printed from a wood-block.
Mid-16th century, English.
Although the pattern of Tudor roses is the same, the
two sections are not identical.
E.73-1910

William Pyne, historian of the Royal Palaces *c.* 1819, records that William Kent, the architect, papered the King's Great Drawing Room at Kensington Palace with the new fangled flock paper; he replaced textile hangings, and thereby set the fashion for flocks, but the pattern survives only in a reconstruction made by Messrs. Bertram in 1909 [plate 14]. The flock papers occupied positions of importance in the main chambers of a house, whilst other papers were hung in the smaller rooms. One of the first wallpaper warehouses, the Blew Paper Warehouse [plate 1] which opened in 1691, specified flock among its papers in an advertisement in *The Postman*, dated December 1702.

The basic method of flocking was to print the block or stencil-cut pattern in an adhesive onto which the powdered wool was sprinkled. Later in the eighteenth century and during the nineteenth century experiments were made to replace powdered pigments for wool, and in due course cotton, silk and lastly nylon cuttings were used as alternatives. A recent development in the process is the spray gun which deposits a flock made from nylon or Perlon onto walls prepared with an adhesive. Though flock has never surpassed the popularity which it enjoyed in the mid-eighteenth century, it has been produced continuously until the present day.

An example of the continuity of a pattern based on a textile design of the first half of the eighteenth century, and reproduced in variant forms in the nineteenth and twentieth centuries, is a large floral flock pattern [plate 15]. Found in several buildings, among them the offices of H.M. Privy Council in the Treasury, Hampton Court Palace and Clandon Park, Surrey, the original was printed in either crimson or dark green. Rarer are flocks which combine two colours, but one colour with a plain background, or a ground with uniform block-printed pattern is found more often, and is exemplified by the floral hanging from St John's College, Cambridge [plate 16].

12
A flock wallpaper.
Early 18th century, English.
From Welwick House, South Lynn, King's Lynn, Norfolk. The pattern is of oak stems and lattice work. On the back is a duty stamp which includes the Royal coat-of-arms, but the heraldry cannot be positively identified. The stamp is of a type hitherto unrecorded, and it is likely to be the first stamp used in the reign of Queen Anne. If this is so, the paper may be dated 1714, as the stamping of papers began on 2 August 1714 and the Queen died on the 7 August in that year.
E.851-1970

13

Panel of flock wallpaper, alternating with a panel of embossed leather.
*c.*1680, English.
From Ivy House, Worcester Cathedral precincts. The whole room from which these panels were taken was decorated in this way with the two alternating patterns. Ivy House was built in 1679, and these wall decorations were found applied directly to the unplastered bricks. The same pattern was found in a flock wallpaper at the Manor House, Saltfleet, Lincolnshire.
E.337-1932

14

A flock wallpaper.
Original 17th century, English.
From the King's Drawing Room, Kensington Palace, London. This reproduction of a 17th-century design was hung when the State Rooms were restored by Messrs. Bertram in 1910. The design is the same as that of a wallpaper in the hall of Bowringsleigh, South Devon, surrounding the Jacobean screen.
E.859-1954

15

Panel of flock wallpaper.
*c.*1735, English.
From the Offices of H. M. Privy Council, London. This paper appears to be the same as that which hung in the Queen's Drawing Room at Hampton Court Palace, and which was removed in 1899 when the mural paintings by Antonio Verrio were found underneath. An Italian brocade of this design and a damask curtain are in the Department of Textiles. The flock was also used at Christchurch Mansion, Ipswich, and at St. Edmund Hall, Oxford.
E.3594-1922

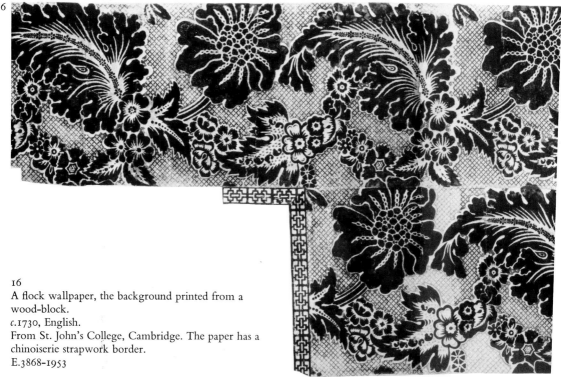

16
A flock wallpaper, the background printed from a
wood-block.
*c.*1730, English.
From St. John's College, Cambridge. The paper has a
chinoiserie strapwork border.
E.3868-1953

The problem of printing wallpaper in more than one colour from wood blocks seems to have been first mastered satisfactorily in this country by John Baptist Jackson, a former employee of the great French manufacturer Réveillon, who began to work in England in the 1740s, printing with oil-based colours [plate 17]. The use of oil-based colours was not Jackson's innovation, as they had been used some years earlier by Jacques Chauvon, an apprentice of Papillon, another French wallpaper manufacturer. Such was Jackson's reputation, however, that almost all early elaborate and colourful pictorial papers were at one time attributed to him. The papers from Doddington Hall, Lincolnshire, from Wallbridge, Gloucestershire [plate 18] and from the Manor House, Bourton-on-the-Water, are printed in distemper colours, not oil-based colour, and are therefore more likely to have come from the workshops of merchants like Thomas Bromwich of The Golden Lion, Ludgate Street, who supplied Horace Walpole at Strawberry Hill in 1754, or Compton and Spinnage of Cockspur Street, who flourished in the 1760s.

Other wallpapers which became very popular were the Chinese, which were introduced into England in the late seventeenth century by Dutch traders and by the East India Company, along with its imports of spices and coffee. These papers were known variously as 'China', 'India', or 'Japan' hangings. An advertisement for an auction sale in 1695 lists Japan hangings and other goods to be sold at the Marine Coffee House, Birchin Lane.

These beautiful, hand-painted wallpapers [plate 19] which decorated a room with non-repeating designs of flowering trees, birds, butterflies, insects, rocks and pots of shrubs, all of authentic naturalistic detail, and with scenes of everyday life in China, were purchased by the wealthy, who sometimes had them mounted on frames so that they could be stored safely, or moved to a new house. The import of Chinese hand-painted wallpaper was continued well into the nineteenth century, supplied by firms of interior decorators like Cowtan & Sons, who obtained the Chinese hangings for Moor Park, Hertfordshire in 1829.

17
Page from an album, with drawings of flowers, foliage and details of ornament.
Mid-18th century, English.
The drawings were used by John Baptist Jackson (1700/01-77) as working material for his wallpaper designs. (J. Kainen, *John Baptist Jackson: 18th Century Master of the Color Woodcut*, Smithsonion Institute Bulletin No. 222, Washington, D.C., 1962).
E.4534-1920

18
A wallpaper printed from chiaroscuro wood-blocks.
*c.*1770, English.
From a house at Wallbridge, Stroud, Gloucestershire. The design consists of architectural pastiches, within rococo scrollwork.
E.50-1971

19
Portion of the base of a wallpaper hand-painted in tempera.
Late 17th century, Chinese.
E.1211-1922

Progress in the manufacture of paper during the seventeenth century and the increase of wealth among the trading classes brought more demand for expensive and luxurious wallpapers, but at the same time cheaper imitative versions of the Chinese papers were made. These specimens of the widespread European taste for exotic Eastern decoration, usually referred to as 'chinoiserie', may often be recognised by their block-printed or etched outlines. An interesting example of crude chinoiserie is from Ord House, Berwick-upon-Tweed, c.1700 [plate 20], where a Chinese figure is placed among plants with an exotic bird and an English red squirrel. A more elegant chinoiserie piece [plate 21] showing a vase of flowers and exotic birds is one of a series, and an early eighteenth-century flock from Hurlecote Manor, Easton Neston [plate 22] also displays chinoiserie motifs in the form of a temple, a pavilion and a 'Chinese' figure.

Styles more expensively carried out in architecture or woodwork were echoed in wallpaper, and this was achieved by chiaroscuro printing from two or more monochrome blocks producing a three dimensional effect of light and shade [plate 23]. The fashion for imitating Gothic architecture, favoured by Horace Walpole at Strawberry Hill, and employed by his friend Thomas Barrett at Lee Priory, is typified by a chiaroscuro ceiling paper, a rare example, from Stubbers, North Ockendon, Essex, which dates from c.1775 [plate 24].

Wharton of Old Park, near Dyrham, a friend of Thomas Grey, refers to 'gilded Gothic paper', mentioning Bromwich as a supplier. An advertisement in *The Postman*, 14 September 1704, stated that the Blew Paper Warehouse sold among other goods, some 'one yard wide emboss'd work in imitation of gilded leather'.

Early eighteenth-century trade cards indicate that many suppliers of wallpaper, such as Joseph and William Marshall of Newgate Street were booksellers and stationers, but the London directories between 1731 and 1780 list over a score of specialist suppliers. The trade cards of these early wallpaper merchants advertise

20
Length of a wallpaper, printed from wood-blocks, with stencilled colour.
c.1700, English.
From Ord House, Berwick-on-Tweed, Northumberland. The paper has been varnished over, either to preserve it, or to give an effect of lacquerwork.
E.5311-1958

21
A panel of wallpaper, printed from etched copperplates, hand-coloured.
1769, English.
The panel is one of a series issued in 1769. Others are at the Museum of London.
E.2001-1919

22
Panel of flock wallpaper.
c.1720, English.
From Hurlcote Manor, Easton Neston, Towcester, Northamptonshire. The condition of the Manor is known back to 1740, at which date this paper was already on the walls.
E.677-1921

23
A panel of ceiling paper, printed from chiaroscuro
wood-blocks.
*c.*1769, English.
From the Old Manor, Bourton-on-the-Water,
Gloucestershire. The paper remained over from the
decoration of the Old Manor in 1769. The circular
border of the design imitates stuccowork.
E.966-1926

24
A panel of ceiling paper, printed from chiaroscuro
wood-blocks.
*c.*1775, English.
From Stubbers, North Ockendon, Essex.
E.91-1937

25
Fragment of a wallpaper printed from wood-blocks, on
a distempered ground.
Late 18th century, English.
From Earls Hall Farmhouse, Prittlewell, Essex.
E.1210-1965

26
Excise Duty stamp with the interlaced monogram of the
Georges. Stamped on the back of a wallpaper from
Wichenford Court, Worcestershire dated *c.*1730-40 [see
plate 10].

24

25

stocks of patterns at least as varied as those available
today, but because wallpaper is semi-ephemeral, relatively few examples of the ordinary cheaper patterns,
produced by the thousand, remain. Those that there are,
are fragmentary, like the graceful but simple rococo
pattern [plate 25], thought suitable to furnish an attic
room in Earls Hall farmhouse, Prittlewell, in the late
eighteenth century. In her diary of 1752 the first Duchess
of Northumberland recorded a visit to Cassiobury Park,
where she saw a vestibule 'fitted up with Prints on a
straw coloured Ground', and in June 1753 Walpole
wrote to Sir Horace Mann describing the furnishings at
Strawberry Hill: 'The room on the ground floor . . .
hung with yellow paper and prints, framed in a new
manner invented by Lord Cardigan, that is with black
and white borders'. The fashion for these 'print rooms'
was adopted in many country houses in the eighteenth
century, among them Woodhall Park, Hertfordshire,

26

---

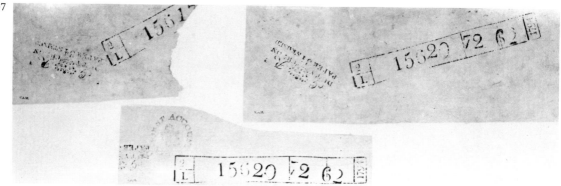

27

Excise Duty stamps: 'First Account Taken' and the 'frame' mark, etc. Stamped on the back of a wallpaper from Cranford House, Middlesex, 1794.

Stratfield Saye, Berkshire, and The Vyne, Hampshire. Both Thomas Chippendale and Matthew Darly provided decors with engraved borders for framing prints, which were pasted to an otherwise plain papered wall. The pattern of a paper from Doddington Hall, Lincolnshire [front cover], seems to have been intended to copy this form of decoration.

Certain instances are known of wallpaper as well as other fittings being specially designed for a house. Accounts for Harewood House show that Chippendale also designed '41 Pieces of the Antique Ornament with Palms &c. on a fine paper with a pink Ground' at a cost of £61 10s, but such references are rare; seventeenth- and eighteenth-century designers of wallpaper are mainly unidentified and exact dating is often a matter of circumstantial evidence found in household accounts.

Much wallpaper was exported to American colonial families in the eighteenth century. A letter written in 1737 by Thomas Hancock of Boston to a London stationer, John Rowe, describes an elaborate paper in the Chinese style which he ordered to be sent to him and referred to a previous order obtained by his friend from Dunbar, a merchant in Aldermanbury. It was customary for a set of wallpapers imported from England to be given as a wedding present from the bridegroom to the bride.

In contrast to the smaller patterns whose designs are related to textiles, are the large panoramic papers. These were enormous in size, (some of the largest measuring 16 metres long by 3 metres high) and were intended to be placed in a sequence on the four walls of a room and illustrated classical stories and scenery. 'Les Monuments de Paris' [plate 28], was produced by Joseph Dufour, Paris, 1814, after designs by Jean Broc, and the 'Cupid and Psyche' legend, by the same manufacturer, required over 1,500 wood blocks to be cut. Some of the scenic wallpapers manufactured by Zuber of Rixheim, for example "El Dorado', were reprinted in editions as late as 1914, and today the American firm A. L. Diament and Co. reproduces several of the great French panoramic sets. Many houses in the United States have scenic wallpapers originally imported in large quantity from France; over two hundred sets of Dufour's 'Les Sauvages de la Mer Pacifique', or 'Voyages of Captain Cook' are to be found, whereas panoramic papers are comparatively rare in Britain.

Some guidance for the dating of wallpaper is given by the stamps impressed on the back of all stained and painted papers by the Excise duty office between 1712 and 1836. Only two stamps are extant which may be dated c.1712-14, as they contain the Stuart coat-of-arms of Queen Anne. From 1714 until 1830 the monogram GR [plate 26] was incorporated in the stamp which had various code numbers, but the key to the numbers is not known. In 1716 an additional circular stamp was brought in to use with the lettering 'First Account Taken', and in 1773 duty was imposed on all imported as well as home-produced papers, with the exception of the Chinese hangings imported by the East India Company. From 1778 onwards, each sheet of paper was ordered to be stamped twice, a stricter measure to avoid evasion of the tax, and in 1786 a 'Duty Charged Remnant' stamp was added, together with a 'frame' mark [plate 27].

22

28
Length of wallpaper printed from wood-blocks.
1814, French.
From a series of thirty pieces, which forms a continuous
panorama of the chief monuments of Paris arranged
along the banks of the Seine. Produced by Dufour
et Leroy after designs by Jean Broc (1780-1850).
E.864-1924

29
Portion of a wallpaper printed from an engraved
copperplate.
Late 17th century, English
The design depicts Diana and Actaeon, Venus and a
satyr. An uncut impression of the engraving is in the
British Museum.
E.901-1924

29

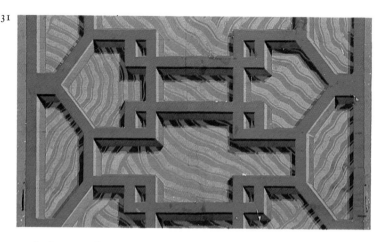

30
Sample piece of a cylinder-printed wallpaper entitled 'King's Star'.
1839, English.
From a record book, probably produced by the firm later known as Jeffrey & Co. The cylinder print is in black on an *irisé* (blended colour) background.
E.431-1943

31
A wallpaper dado, printed from wood-blocks.
1820, English.
From the Royal Pavilion, Brighton. Designed by Robert Jones, (also a designer of furniture, a mural painter and decorator), who collaborated with Crace in the work on the interior of the Pavilion with its exotic chinoiserie schemes.
E.9849-1958

The frame mark, instances of which are comparatively few, conveniently contains the year of manufacture in the right-hand section of the stamp. In 1792 the tax was extended to include Chinese papers. An import stamp may also be found on some papers with the name of a depot, for example 'Customs G R Paper Ipswich'. On the 5 July 1836 the statutes decreeing the taxation of home produced wallpapers were repealed, but imported papers continued to be taxed until 1861.

From applications made to the Patent Office we know of attempts to use machinery in wallpaper printing as far back as 1692 when Bayley's patent was approved for 'printing all sorts of Paper . . . with several engines made of Brasse and such like other Mettals, with Fire . . .' Many other experiments were tried, which for one reason or another were not permanently adopted. The seventeenth-century engraved wallpaper 'Diana and Actaeon' [plate 29] which is uncoloured, and a series of etched chinoiserie panels produced in 1769, were presumably made by a method similar to that employed by Edward Dighton who applied for a patent in 1753 for printing wallpaper by etched or engraved plates impressed by a rolling mill; papers so printed were then to be hand-coloured. In 1792 A. G. Eckhardt, whose factory was in Sloane Street, Chelsea, took out a patent for a variant process of engraved copperplate printing; his factory's floral wallpapers were noted for their beauty and high quality. Wallpaper was printed by hand-operated cylinders at least as early as 1764, when Thomas Fryer obtained his patent for printing several kinds of textiles and paper. Until the early part of the nineteenth century paper was produced only in hand-made sheets, the largest of which was the 'double demy' twelve of which pasted together formed a strip (roughly 10·5 m × 53·3 cm, in imperial 11½ yards × 21 inches), on which wallpaper could be printed. In 1799 a Frenchman, Louis Robert, constructed a small model machine capable of making continuous lengths of paper, an invention developed in England on a full-sized machine by the Fourdrinier brothers, c.1801-1803. In 1816 Edward Cooper invented a machine which could print from curved stereotyped plates, on the 'continuous' paper which was available from about 1806, though its use for printing wallpaper was not permitted by the

Excise authorities prior to 1830. In 1835 came Thomas Greig's machine for colour printing and embossing from three separate metal cylinders geared into register, and in 1839 Joseph Birche's process of drying rapidly-printed paper was in operation. In the same year Harold Potter of the Darwen wallpaper factory patented a power-driven roller machine adapted from Bell's calico printer. It printed from engraved metal rollers from which the surplus colour was removed by a doctor blade. The age of mass production of wallpaper by power-driven machinery now began [plate 59]. Nevertheless the best quality wallpaper was still made by the hand block printing process, which continues to be used by specialist firms today, but for the most part since the 1950s relief printing methods from wood blocks have been replaced by silkscreen, rotagravure and the techniques of flexigraphic printing and ink embossing. The latter process, invented by Heidemann, was first used in this country in the 1960s.

Until about the middle of the nineteenth century only natural dyestuffs were available, but in 1856 an English chemist, W. H. Perkins, prepared the first aniline dye from the distillation of coal tar. This produced a mauve dye, but the production of other colours from this process soon followed. Aniline dyes contain a certain amount of arsenious acid, or white arsenic, but the most toxic preparation used in industry was Scheele's green, or arsenic of copper. The arsenical compounds were made to adhere to paper by size which when drying released particles into the air that could be inhaled.

'In 1861, an inquest was held in London on one of four children who had licked green paper-hangings, and the evidence was so strong that the Court hesitated to receive a verdict of natural death', *Universal Decorator*, 1861. The use of arsenical paints and wallpaper pigments was the subject of much discussion and controversy during the second half of the nineteenth century. It is said that the watercolour painter E. H. Corbould was taken ill whilst on a job at Osborne House, which caused Queen Victoria to order the examination of the wallpaper in his bedroom and this was found to contain much arsenic. In 1862 an investigation into the conditions of child employment in the wallpaper industry further publicised the problem of toxic colour. William Woollams & Co., having discovered a substitute for the arsenic emerald green pigment, ceased to use it, and by the 1870s Jeffrey & Co. were advertising their products as 'arsenic free'. Eventually all the leading manufacturers, including Morris & Co., followed their example.

It is easy to associate the nineteenth century with the most bizarre and ill-conceived patterns, produced to demonstrate the versatility of the machine rather than the rules of good design, but rich and varied patterns of a high quality made from hand-carved blocks, as well as simple and attractive cylinder prints [plate 30], can be seen in the pattern books of the first half of that century.

Two names of interior designers which emerge at the beginning of the nineteenth century are J. G. Crace and Thomas Willement. Crace [plate 31] who worked at Windsor Castle and the Royal Pavilion, Brighton, for the Prince Regent, was also associated with A. W. N. Pugin in the decoration of the new Houses of Parliament [plate 32]. The Crace firm's stock eventually passed to Cowtan & Sons giving them a range of interior designs which dated from the eighteenth century, and their wallpaper order books, now at the V & A, cover the years from 1824 to 1938. They contain thousands of patterns supplied to large and small establishments throughout Britain, and are of outstanding interest to scholars and restorers of old buildings because of their references to specific locations and dates. Thomas Willement, an architect, decorator and stained glass

32
A wallpaper, printed from wood-blocks.
1847, English.
Designed by A. W. N. Pugin (1812-52) for the Houses of Parliament, produced by Samuel Scott for J. G. Crace. The initials incorporated in the design are 'V R' [Victoria Regina].
E.150-1976

32

33
Wallpaper frieze printed from chiaroscuro wood-blocks, with machine-printed background.
*c.*1851, English.
Probably part of an eight-metre-long frieze of the Elgin marbles, exhibited by Jeffrey, Allen & Co. at the Great Exhibition, 1851.
E.33B-1971

designer, designed wallpapers and carpets for Alton Towers, Staffordshire and for Charlecote House, Warwickshire; some orders for these houses appear in the Cowtan volumes.

Both Owen Jones, author of *The Grammar of Ornament*, 1856, and William Morris, the craftsman and mediaevalist, objected to the imitation of woodwork

and other forms of art and craft in pattern designing [plate 33]. Morris maintained that as the purpose of wallpaper is to cover flat surfaces, the only legitimate form of design for it should be two dimensional in appearance. Jones who designed a great deal of wallpaper consistently produced abstract or semi-abstract versions of leaf and flower forms, but Morris achieved a rich and subtle blend of natural shapes within the framework of formal design. He had attempted unsuccessfully to print his own wallpapers from metal plates, and handed over the designs to Jeffrey & Co., whose first production, 'The Daisy' [plate 34], 1864, was one of the simplest of his wallpapers, and one which retained its popularity. More intricate and magnificent

34
Wallpaper printed from wood-blocks, entitled 'The Daisy'.
1864, English.
Designed by William Morris (1834-96), produced by Jeffrey & Co. This was the second wallpaper that Morris designed, but the first to be issued.
E.441-1919

35
Wallpaper printed from wood-blocks, entitled 'Acanthus'.
1875, English.
Designed by William Morris (1834-96), produced by Jeffrey & Co.
Circ. 281-1959

36
Panel of wallpaper printed from wood-blocks, entitled
'La Margarete', with the 'Alcestis' frieze.
1876, English.
Designed by Walter Crane, R.W.S. (1845-1915),
produced by Jeffrey & Co. The paper was shown at the
Philadelphia Exhibition of 1876.
E.1837-1934

37
A flock wallpaper, with a block-printed background.
1872, English. *219470*
Designed by William Burges, A.R.A. (1827-81),
produced by Jeffrey & Co. The paper with the dado
and frieze to be used with it are illustrated in the
*Building News*, 11 October 1872.
E.97-1955

38
Watercolour design for a wallpaper with bamboo leaves
and formalised Japanese flowers.
1872 English.
Designed by Edward W. Godwin, F.S.A. (1833–66),
produced by Jeffrey & Co.
E.515-1963

39
Panel of a wallpaper printed with flock, and wood-blocks.
1877, English.
Designed by Bruce J. Talbert (1838-81), produced by Jeffrey & Co. The main design of this wallpaper was shown in the Paris Exhibition of 1878.
E.1842-1934

40
Design for a wallpaper. Watercolour.
*c*.1855, English.
By Owen Jones (1809-74).
D.762-1897

41
Panel of a wallpaper, printed from engraved rollers.
1895, English.
Produced by David Walker.
E.1943-1967

are 'The Acanthus' [plate 35], 1875, and the 'St. James's', 1881, the latter designed for the Throne Room and the Wellington Room in St. James's Palace. Morris gave his advice to designers in the following words:

> I think the real way to deal successfully with designing for paper hangings is to accept their mechanical nature frankly, to avoid falling into the trap of trying to make your paper look as if it were painted by hand. Here is the place, if anywhere, for dots and lines and hatchings; mechanical enrichment is of the first necessity in it.

Nevertheless, the absence in the printed version of the white dotted line on the edges of the leaf shown in Morris' original watercolour design for 'The Acanthus' suggests that on this occasion he may have taken the advice of the block cutter and chosen a less ornate finish than he had first intended for this paper.

Metford Warner, who joined Jeffrey & Co. in 1866, and was inspired by Morris's work adopted a policy of commissioning artists and architects, among them Walter Crane [plate 36], William Burges [plate 37], E. W. Godwin [plate 38] and C. L. Eastlake to design

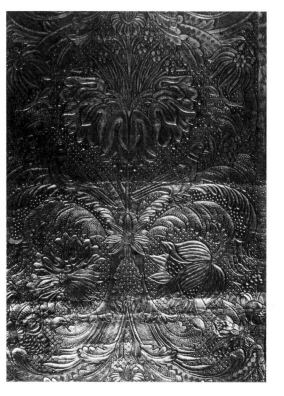

42
A wallpaper embossed to simulate leather.
Early 20th century, Japanese.
Produced by Alexander Rottmann & Co.'s factory in
Japan.
E.479-1967

43
A nursery wallpaper, machine-printed, with a
representation of the Four Seasons.
Probably c.1860, English.
E.1114-1921

wallpapers for his firm. Warner won admission for wallpaper for the first time to the Fine Arts Exhibition, held
at the Albert Hall in 1873.

Also on Jeffrey & Co.'s list of designers were Bruce J.
Talbert [plate 39], Owen Jones [plate 40] and Brightwen
Binyon; together with Godwin, Crane and Burges,
they all designed a type of paper made popular by the
firm in the 1870s, which consisted of a combined frieze,
or top border, filling, or main stretch of pattern, and
dado, or lower division of the wall, in a single printing.
Angled versions were made for staircase walls.

Varnished grounds, intended to make wallpaper more
durable, were produced in the eighteenth century.
They were also used with the purpose of making
paperhangings washable, for in 1802 Crease of Bath
advertised a varnish after-process for this purpose.
The first form of manufacture which created a semi-
washable product, by printing from engraved metal
plates in transparent oils or varnish colours, was
pioneered by the Manchester firm of Heywood,
Higginbotham Smith in 1871. The new papers were
known as 'sanatories' [plate 41] and had a stippled or

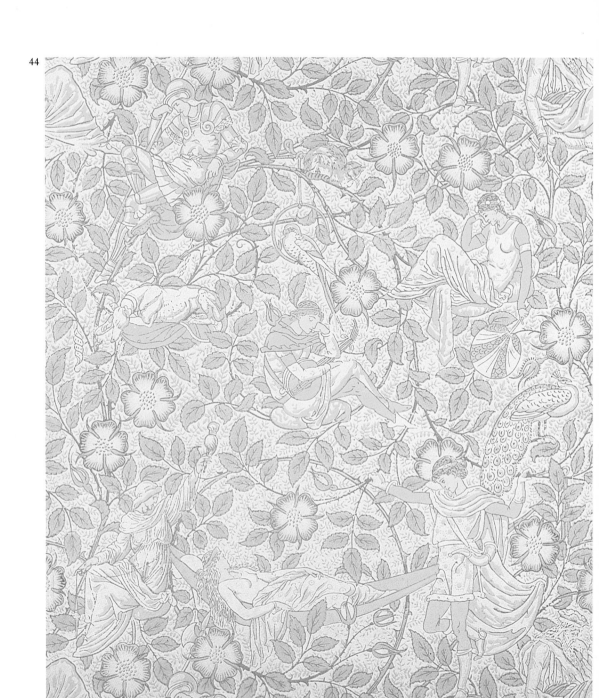

44
A nursery wallpaper, machine-printed, entitled 'The
Sleeping Beauty'.
1879, English.
Designed by Walter Crane, R.W.S. (1845-1915),
produced by Jeffrey & Co.
Circ. 566-1931

45
A nursery wallpaper, machine-printed.
*c.*1900, English.
Adapted by J. Cheetham Cockshut from illustrations in Randolph Caldecott's *Nursery Books*, produced by Allen, Cockshut & Co.
E.1825-1934

grainy appearance capable of a delicate shading effect, which is distinguishable from work produced from blocks printing dots off metal pins, a process in use from the latter part of the eighteenth century.

The embossing of paper is described in the *Universal Dictionary of Trade and Commerce*, 1751. In Robert Mylne's diary of 1768 he says 'With Mr Southwell to Mr Bromwich for choice of papier mache'. Embossed paper must have been commonly used in the eighteenth century as it is described in advertisements of the period, though little appears to have survived. Patents were granted to John G. Hancock for embossing and chasing paper, 1796, to Thomas Cobb, 1829, and to Thomas de la Rue, 1834, for an emboss in parallel lines running only along the length of the paper to give the effect of light playing on the surface. The nineteenth century patents for various textures in wallpaper are too numerous to list here, but mention should be made of Kurz's patent in France in 1842 for a shallow-embossing machine, which produced among other textures an imitation of moiré silk. Although the method of fine embossing by engraved, heated metal plates dates back to the eighteenth century, samples of a cruder, less visually effective imitation of silk by wood block printing are found in the pattern books of the 1820s and 1830s.

Pictorial papers, both large and small, had been produced at least since the early eighteenth century, but none seems to have been specifically intended for nursery decoration until the first half of the nineteenth century. A fragment of a cylinder-printed pattern of the 1840s depicting comic characters and scenes, with a figure of Mr Punch, found in a London house recently, is probably the oldest surviving specimen of an English wallpaper indisputably intended for the nursery. A trellis pattern with vignettes of 'The Four Seasons' [plate 43] may be dated to *c.*1860. Walter Crane, who gained his reputation as an illustrator of children's books, designed his first nursery paper for Jeffrey & Co., 'The Queen of Hearts' in 1875. A subsequent design 'The Sleeping Beauty'

46
A nursery wallpaper border and frieze, hand-painted flock.
*c.*1930, English.
Produced by A. Sanderson & Sons Ltd, and based on the Disney Studios 'Mickey Mouse' cartoons.
E.3100-1930

47
A nursery wallpaper, screenprinted.
1957, English.
Designed by Christine Risley,
produced by the Wallpaper
Manufacturers Ltd., in their
'Palladio' range.
E.893-1978

[plate 44], 1879, which was exhibited at the International Health Exhibition in 1884 is one of the most charming papers ever made for the nursery. Many machine-printed papers which were cheap and washable, notably Kate Greenaway's 'The Months', 1893, were available in the second half of the nineteenth century, and the works of other illustrators, including Randolph Caldecott [plate 45], Mabel L. Attwell, Cecil Aldin, John Hassall and Will Owen were the subject of some of the best-loved friezes and wallpapers for children of the period. A frieze based on drawings by Beatrix Potter produced early in the twentieth century remained a favourite for sixty years. Related to nursery papers and often used in the nursery were the Victorian commemorative papers. Brightly coloured, instructive, they celebrated events ranging from Wellington's victories to scenes from Derby Day and the Boat Race. A typical twentieth-century design of the period after the First World War is the border with Mickey Mouse theme [plate 46], produced by A. Sanderson Sons, c.1930. An attractive paper of the 1950s is Christina Risley's 'Joanna' [plate 47], c.1957. Shand Kydd devoted sections of their 'focus' series of pattern books of the 1960s to designs for the nursery or playroom, and one of their most attractive nursery wallpapers is based on Peggy Fortnum's illustrations to Michael Bond's 'Paddington Bear' stories. 'Crown wallpaper' produced papers which encompassed the interests of children of the period in soldiers, aeroplanes, vintage cars and the current mythologies of spacemen and 'The Flintstones'.

In the past, doors, often decorative features in themselves, were not normally wallpapered, but a recent innovation to the decoration of the nursery or playroom, the 'Photodoor', a photogravure mural, depicting such

48
A wallpaper frieze, hand-stencilled.
1896, English.
Designed by William Shand Kydd (1864-1936),
produced by Shand Kydd Ltd.
E.1524-1954

characters as Snoopy or the Muppets, is designed to cover the plain modern flush door.

In the last quarter of the nineteenth century, under the influence of the Aesthetic Movement, many wallpapers were designed to complement the Japanese style in furniture and accessories; Bruce J. Talbert and E. W. Godwin were leading exponents of this style. Simultaneously by the early 1900s large flamboyant art nouveau patterns were in the height of fashion [plate 48], and the designers of wallpaper who represented English art nouveau best were Arthur Gwatkin [plate 49], George Walton [plate 50], C. F. A. Voysey [plate 51], and Harry Napper [plate 52].

The wallpaper market was not, of course, entirely dominated by art nouveau designs at this time and included the traditional floral fillings and naturalistic friezes. Shand Kydd Ltd., founded in 1885, had revived the art of stencilling in their friezes, which combined both block printing and delicate stencilled shading. The Silver Studios, founded in 1880 by Arthur Silver and continued by his son Rex [plate 53] supplied designs of conventionalised flower and plant subjects to Lightbown, Aspinall & Co. between 1893 and 1898, and to Alexander Rottmann, who exhibited the friezes 'The Argosies' and 'The Thicket' which won praise at Rottmann's exhibition in 1895. Rottmann's Yokohoma factory in Japan later produced the series entitled 'The Silvern Stencils'. The Silver Studios also supplied designs to Libertys and to Alexander Morton's textile firm; Arthur Silver's declared purpose for his firm was 'to provide designs for the whole field of fabrics and other materials used in the decoration of the house'.

Another society, the Century Guild, founded in 1882 by A. H. Mackmurdo and Selwyn Image, aimed to 'render all branches of art the sphere no longer of the tradesman but of the artist', and numbered among its members Herbert Horne, who joined as Mackmurdo's pupil in 1883. He designed a series of distinctive patterns, including the large wallpaper frieze and filling, 'The Bay Leaf' [plate 54] produced by Jeffrey & Co., and shown at the Inventions Exhibition in 1885.

49

38

49
A hall wallpaper, machine-printed from engraved rollers.
*c.*1903, English.
Designed by Arthur Gwatkin, produced by Wylie & Lochhead.
E.467-1967

50
Wallpaper, machine-printed.
1905, English.
Designed by George Walton (1867-1933), produced by Jeffrey & Co.
E.2348-1932

51
Watercolour design for a wallpaper entitled 'Isis'.
*c.*1895, English.
Designed by Charles F. A. Voysey (1857-1941), produced by Jeffrey & Co.
E.39-1945

52
A wallpaper, machine-printed, entitled 'The Braunton'.
*c.*1902, Engiish.
Designed by Harry Napper (d. 1930), produced by
Alexander Rottmann & Co. Napper managed the
Silver Studios for a while after Arthur Silver's death in
1896.
E.641-1971

53
Wallpaper frieze, stencil.
*c.*1905, English.
Designed by Rex Silver (1879–1965), produced by John
Line & Sons Ltd.
Circ. 590–1967

54
A wallpaper and frieze printed from wood blocks,
entitled 'The Bay Leaf'.
*c.*1882, English.
Designed by Herbert Horne (1864-1916), produced by
Jeffrey & Co.
E.966-1978

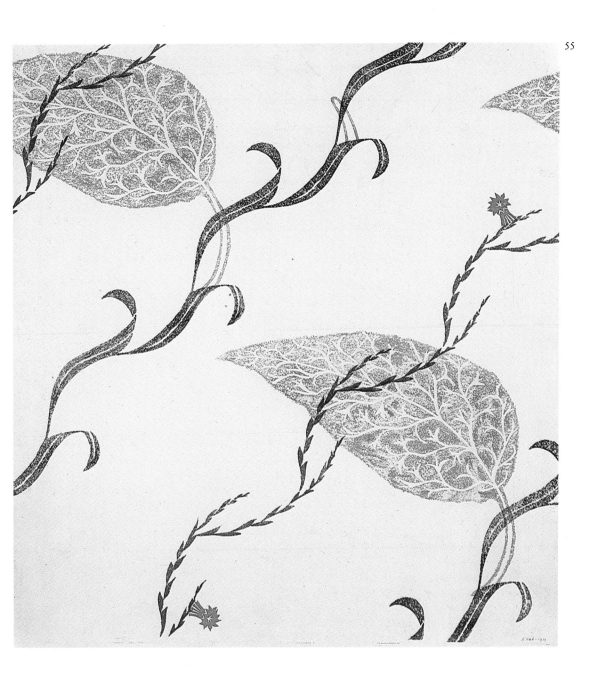

55
A wallpaper, printed by lithography.
*c.*1930, English.
Designed by Edward Bawden (1900), printed and
published by the Curwen Press Ltd.
E.546-1931

A wallpaper, screen-printed.
1951, English.
Designed by Robert Sevant, produced by John Line &
Sons Ltd.
E.888-1978

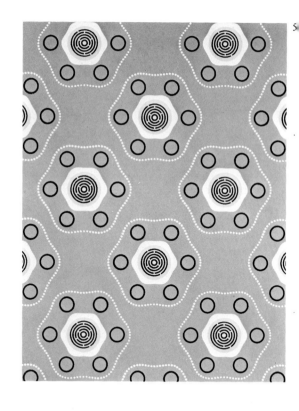

The Wallpaper Manufacturers Ltd. was formed by some of the best-known firms in 1899 as a joint stock company to give financial support to smaller firms still using hand-printing methods. After the Second World War they launched their 'Lancastria' collection, principally to promote exports to America. These papers, which were semi-washable, led to the production of washable papers as a standard in the following years.

After the 1914-1918 War, which had halted wallpaper production, the papers of the 1920s and 1930s were for the most part either in the traditional styles with emphasis on the Tudor revival, or in the modern art deco style. The influence of the craft revivalists of the 1930s is strongly expressed in Edward Bawden's wallpapers [plate 55], which were printed directly from his linocuts by Cole & Son, and lithographically reproduced by the Curwen Press Ltd.

In the 1950s in America, the idea of wallpaper as a feature for 'random' walls, or single panels, was developed; screenprinted panels after designs by Matisse, Joan Miró and Alexander Calder are among those illustrated in L. & W. Katzenbach's *The Practical Book of American Wallpaper*, Philadelphia, 1951.

In England in the 1950s Sandersons had begun to reprint from the William Morris wood blocks, which came into their possession when Morris Co. was dissolved c.1941. Among their reprints are designs by J. H. Dearle, May Morris, and the later Morris Co. productions.

In 1950 the Council of Industrial Design issued a series of folios, one of which contained a selection of approved contemporary designs in wallpaper, with advice on the choice of patterns for small rooms; among the manufacturers represented in the folio were Cole & Son, Sandersons, John Line and Shand Kydd.

The molecular structure of natural objects seen under microphotography had considerable influence on the design style of the 1950s [plate 56], a collection of patterns based on the crystalline structure of insulin, afwillite, myglobin, etc. was shown at the Festival of Britain in 1951. In this year John Line brought out the first British screenprinted wallpaper in 'Limited

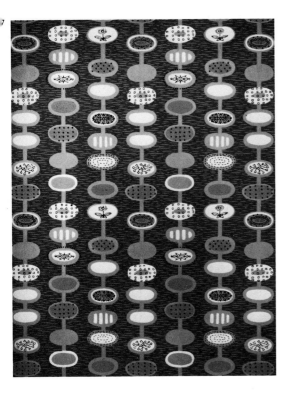

57
A wallpaper, screen-printed, entitled 'Provence'.
1951, English.
Designed by Lucienne Day (born 1917), produced by
John Line & Sons Ltd., in their series 'Limited Editions'.
F.569-1966

Editions 1951', which contained the work of John Minton, Jacqueline Groag, Sylvia Priestley and Lucienne Day [plate 57].

In 1956 the Wallpaper Manufacturers produced their first 'Palladio' series, which presented the public with a new set of fresh designs by young artists. The series thrived and a typical example from the 'Palladio' 8 pattern book of 1968, (Wallpaper Manufacturers' first screen-printed vinyl papers) is Judith Cash's 'Impact' [plate 58].

Advances in photographic printing led to photo-murals and the increased production of photogravure wallpaper with the naturalistic 'brickwall' pattern decorating coffee houses and bars in the 1960s. Shand Kydd Ltd., which merged with John Line in 1958, began to produce its own original line of designs with the first of the series of 'Focus' pattern books, 1964-1965. The emphasis throughout this volume was in making the papers resemble fabric, linen, silk, hessian or textured cotton. A review in *The Decorator* commented on 'Focus' that 'for the first time a costly photo-gravure machine, similar to that used in magazine work, has been used to create facsimiles of artists' works. Designs now look like screenprinted papers but cost less than half the price'. A design by Donald Melbourne, 'Festival', is probably the first example in this country of printing by the Heidemann ink-embossing machinery.

The 1970s have seen a renewed interest in the small patterns of the early nineteenth century, and for matching fabrics and wallpapers; firms such as Osborne and Little, The Designers Guild Ltd., and Laura Ashley, the textile designer, who extended her range to paints and wallpapers in 1975, manufacture these. The increasing interest in the restoration of historic interiors, for example, and the demand of concerns like the National Trust, has resulted in the reprinting or reproduction of wallpapers dating from the seventeenth to the early twentieth century.

Wall papers are used as often today in room decoration as at any previous period, and with the combination of historic revivals and new designs are set to continue making an important contribution to the contemporary interior.

58
A wallpaper, screen-printed entitled 'Impact'.
1968, English.
Designed by Judith Cash, produced by the Wallpaper
Manufacturers Ltd., in their 'Palladio' series.
E.5134-1968

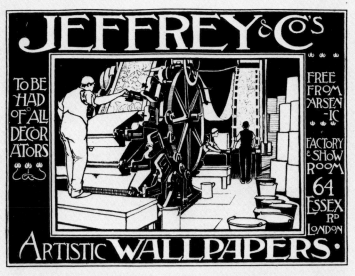

64, ESSEX ROAD,
ISLINGTON, · LONDON, N.
*SPRING,* 1899.

DEAR SIR,

WE have pleasure in forwarding to you our **NEW BOOK OF INEXPENSIVE WALL-PAPERS,** all of which are KEPT IN STOCK DURING THE SEASON. The Book forms a complete collection of carefully selected Papers suited for the entire decoration of a house.

For Special Work we can forward on Loan our

**NEW STAND BOOK** of finest **HAND-PRINTED** and **EMBOSSED WALL-PAPERS,** many of which are Kept in Stock.

**A SMALL BOOK** of **INEXPENSIVE HAND-PRINTED PAPERS.**

**A BOOK** of **STAIRCASE DECORATIONS.**

**NEW SERIES** of **RAISED FLOCKS** for **WALLS** and **CEILINGS.**

**NEW SERIES** of **COLOURED FLOCKS** for **DINING** and **DRAWING ROOMS.**

**CEILING PAPERS** in **PLAIN COLOURS.** **CEILING PAPERS** in **"RELIEVO"** for **PAINTING.**

ALSO

**THE SPECIAL BOOK OF DAMASKS AND CHINTZES.**

THE SPECIAL BOOK OF **WALL-PAPERS** designed by **HEYWOOD SUMNER.**

Yours faithfully,

THE HIGHEST AWARDS AT ALL INTERNATIONAL EXHIBITIONS

EXCELLENCY OF DESIGN AND SUPERIORITY OF COLOURING AND WORKMANSHIP.

JEFFREY & CO.

P.S. In writing for Loan Patterns please say which of the above are required.

59
Letter-heading of Jeffrey & Co., showing multicolour
wallpaper printing machinery.
1899, English.
E.42A(2)-1945

# Further Reading

A. V. Sugden's and E. L. Edmondson's *A History of English Wallpaper 1509-1914* remains the classic well-illustrated work, although it was published by B. T. Batsford Ltd. as long ago as 1925, and its account ceases before the first War; it is unique in containing 'mill records' and historical notes on the major wallpaper manufacturers. Since its publication more research has been carried out, notably on the earlier history of wallpaper: a pioneering study was Hilary Jenkinson's article 'English Wallpapers of the Sixteenth and Seventeenth Centuries' in the *Antiquaries Journal*, 1925. In 1929 the Department of Engraving, Illustration and Design of the V&A published a *Catalogue of Wallpapers*, which contained an excellent, comprehensive, historical account by Charles Oman, now reprinted in the revision of the catalogue published by Philip Wilson Ltd in 1982. For the general reader, as well as the student of the subject, the following works by Eric A. Entwisle are recommended:

*A Literary History of Wallpaper*, B. T. Batsford Ltd., London, 1960
*Wallpapers of the Victorian Era*, Frank Lewis, Leigh-on-Sea, 1964
*The Book of Wallpaper: a history and an appreciation*, 2nd edition, Kingsmead, Bath, 1970
*French Scenic Wallpapers*, Frank Lewis, Leigh-on-Sea, 1972

A bibliography, originally compiled by Mr Entwisle as a supplement to the catalogue of the 'Exhibition of Historical and British Wallpapers' held at the Suffolk Galleries, London, May 1945, has been updated by him and is included in the revised V & A catalogue.

A general work by Brenda Greysmith, *Wallpaper*, Studio Vista, London, 1976, has amassed a large amount of information relating to the history and manufacture of the materials which were the forerunners to wallpapers in England, Europe and America. In her book emphasis is given to the social and industrial aspects of the subject.

Henri Clouzot's and C. Follot's *Histoire du Papier Peint en France*, Editions D' Art Charles Moreau, Paris, 1935 and *Le Papier Peint en France du XVIIe au XIXe siècle*, Les Editions G. Van Oest, Paris, 1931, are standard French texts, while H. Olligs's 3 volume *Tapeten, Ihre Geschichte bis zur Gegenwart*, Klinkhardt & Biermann, Braunschweig, 1969-70, covers the history of wallpaper to the present day. Volume 3 is largely descriptive of the technical history of manufacture, and the work is completed with very full indices and bibliography.

Two books on specific aspects of the subject may be recommended: A. V. Sugden's and E. A. Entwisle's *Potters of Darwen, 1839-1939, A Century of Wallpaper Printing by Machinery*, G. Falkner & Sons, Manchester, 1939, and Fiona Clark's *William Morris Wallpapers and Chintzes*, St. Martin's Press, New York, & Academy Editions, London, 1974.

For those especially interested in the origins of wallpaper, Horst Appuhn's and Christian V. Heusinger's *Riesenholzschnitte und Papiertapeten der Renaissance*, Verlag Dr. Alfons Uhl, Unterschneidheim, 1976 gives an account of the earliest known European wallpapers.

## DATE DUE

| | | | |
|---|---|---|---|
| | | | |
| | | | |
| | | | |
| | | | |
| | | | |
| | | | |
| | | | |
| | | | |
| | | | |
| | | | |
| | | | |
| | | | |
| | | | |
| | | | |
| | | | |
| | | | |
| | | | |
| | | | |
| GAYLORD | | | PRINTED IN U.S.A. |